All Charged Up!

Elizabeth Massie

Contents

Rigby

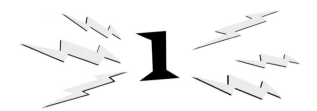

Energy: It's Everywhere!

Imagine that you're at home making popcorn and listening to music on the radio. You're holding a mystery book that you're eager to begin reading. Suddenly there is a flash of lightning and a crash of thunder outside. It doesn't occur to you that this thunderstorm may ruin your evening plans.

But then—in the stillness—you realize that you don't hear the popcorn popping or the music playing anymore, and you can't even see your book. You're surrounded by darkness, you're hungry, and now you can't read your mystery. What's happened?

 Lightning might interrupt the flow of electricity to your home or city by breaking an electric power line.

The flow of **electricity** that powers your home has been stopped—but how? Maybe lightning hit a tree and it fell over, snapping the power line, or perhaps a strong wind knocked the power line down. Whatever it was, your **energy** source is gone, and now you wonder what you're going to do.

 Many homes and businesses in the United States use electric energy.

You may have to call the power company and ask them to send out a crew with special equipment to fix the broken line. While you're waiting, you might start thinking about all of the things in your home that won't run without energy from the power company.

As you sit in your dark, silent home, trying to read your book with a flashlight, you might even begin to wonder—what is energy, anyway?

Energy is the power of certain forces in nature to do work, and it can warm a cup of cocoa, freeze an ice cube, light your room, or run an electric car.

Different kinds of electric machines change electricity in different ways, and you have probably seen or experienced machines that produce:

- light
- sound
- heat
- electromagnetism.

Energy is everywhere. All you have to do is look around, and you'll find it!

Energy powers a Ferris wheel to carry you and your friends on an exciting ride.

The sun can be used for energy, too. How does your family dry laundry? Many people put their wet clothes into an electric dryer, but that's not the only way to get the job done. If you want to save money on your power bill, you could hang your wet laundry outdoors and let the sun dry it for free!

Can we trap the sun's power—or **solar energy**—to produce other forms of energy to use in our everyday lives? The answer is *yes,* and many people are doing this today!

Heat energy from the sun can dry your wet laundry.

Did You Know?
- *Sol* in Spanish means *sun.*
- *Solar* in English means *of or from the sun!*

You may have seen shiny solar panels on a building. These solar panels trap energy from the sun so that its power can be used for many of the same things that are often powered by electricity.

This building has solar panels on its roof that collect the sun's energy and change it into other forms of energy needed inside.

2

So, What Is Electricity, Anyway?

Have you ever seen a flash of lightning streak across the sky? Have you ever dragged your feet across a rug, touched someone's arm, and felt a spark jump from your finger to his or her body? If you have, you've experienced electricity.

Electricity is a kind of energy that is found in nature. In the last 100 years or so, people have learned how to use electricity to run all kinds of machines. We use electricity every day because it makes our lives easier.

 Electricity powers the headphones, screen, and keyboard of the special computer this blind child is using.

How Do We Use Electricity?

Electricity is one of the most useful forms of energy in the world. More than 100 million homes in the United States use electricity to operate appliances, tools, and other items.

Have you ever noticed the power lines stretching high above the streets in your neighborhood? These are the cables that carry electricity over long distances from power companies to customers' homes, schools, and businesses.

Electricity can travel many miles through power lines supported on steel towers.

If you search through your home, you'll find several objects that use electricity. Many of them have cords that are plugged into wall sockets. In the kitchen, you might find a refrigerator, a microwave, and a coffeemaker, and in the bedroom, you might find a radio, an alarm clock, and a lamp. What electrically-powered things could you find in the living room?

Some machines that use electricity produce light, while others produce sound. Some heat your food and some cool it down. This means electricity can do many different kinds of work for us.

Electricity creates the heat a microwave uses to warm up your food.

How Does Electricity Work?

Electricity is one of our basic forms of energy. It is made of tiny, moving particles that can jump through the air and move smoothly without being seen.

Have you ever used a garden hose to water plants? Water flows through the hose until you turn it off. An electric current, or the flow of electricity, works in much the same way, except that it travels in a circular path called a **circuit.**

A circuit is the way electricity travels to a machine or an appliance. Once the electricity arrives, the appliance works by changing electricity into light, sound, heat, or electromagnetism. Every time you turn on an electrical appliance, you're creating a circuit that works in this way. . . .

A Simple Circuit

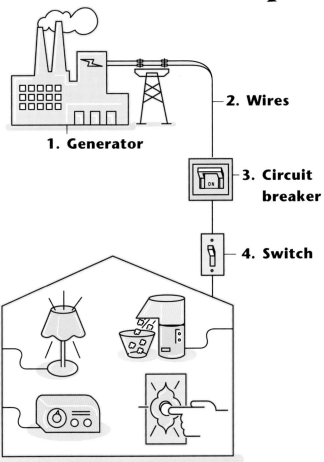

2. Wires

1. Generator

3. Circuit breaker

4. Switch

1. A **generator,** such as a power plant, creates electricity and sends it to your home.

2. Electricity flows from the generator through wires until it is stopped by something, such as a circuit breaker. If too much electricity flows into your home at once, a circuit breaker will stop it.

3. When the circuit breaker is turned on, electricity can flow into your home for you to use.

4. When an appliance is plugged in and its switch is turned on, the circuit is complete, or unbroken, and electricity can reach the appliances. Suddenly the lightbulb glows and the radio plays. The popcorn popper hums and the doorbell rings!

3

Turn on the Lights!

What do you do when it gets dark at the end of the day? If you're like most people, you probably turn on the lights. It's hard to imagine living without electric lights, but for thousands of years everyone did. Candles, torches, and oil lamps provided some light, but not nearly enough to help us read or work. Often when the sun went down, people simply went to sleep.

 The world would be very different at night if we had no sources of light. What are some things we would not be able to do?

1920s

2000

All of that changed completely when the lightbulb that we use today was invented by Thomas Edison in 1879. Before long people were able to read, work—and even play baseball—at night.

Lightbulbs today do work better and last longer than the lightbulb Edison invented, but how they work remains the same: They are simple devices for changing electrical energy into light energy.

Since their invention, lightbulbs have helped to brighten up rooms at night or on cloudy days.

15

What Is Light?

Light is a kind of energy that helps our eyes see things. Light travels in straight lines, and if it hits a dark surface, such as a purple sweater, much of it will be absorbed, or trapped. However, if it hits a mirror, it is reflected, or bounced off. And if it hits a clear glass window, it can travel right through!

Natural light comes mainly from the sun. Artificial light produced by a lightbulb is not exactly the same as natural light, but it is similar. It allows you to light up your home when the sun goes down just by turning on a switch!

 When light hits an object, the light may be absorbed by the object, bounce off of it, or pass right through!

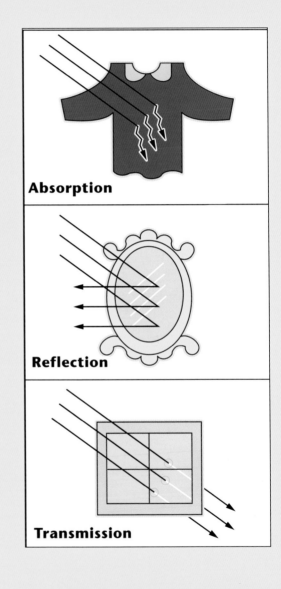

Absorption

Reflection

Transmission

16

How Does a Lightbulb Work?

A lightbulb is made of three parts: a base, a series of wires, and a glass bulb. The lightbulb is part of an electrical circuit that begins at the electric company's power plant. When you turn on the switch, you complete the circuit and the lightbulb lights up.

The wires in the lightbulb are made of a material that carries electricity. When electricity passes through the wires, the little particles inside the electricity bump up and rub against each other. Have you ever rubbed your hands together on a cold day? You're using **friction** to warm up. When the particles in electricity bump against each other, they create friction, too, heating the thin wire and making it glow, creating light.

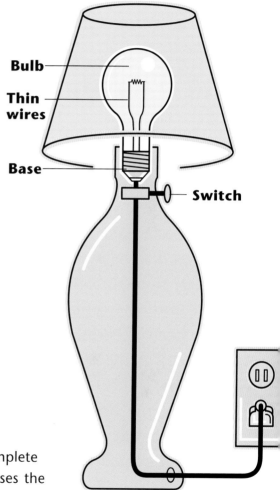

 When a lamp switch is turned on, the circuit is complete and electricity flows through the lamp. Friction causes the filament to heat up and glow, producing light.

4

Did You Hear That Sound?

Imagine that you're alone in your bedroom, and it's very quiet. . . . In fact, it's too quiet, so you reach out and turn on an appliance, and suddenly your room is filled with music! You turn the dial and hear people talking, then turn it again until the sound of a crowd cheering at a baseball game reaches your ears. What is this machine that brings so many different sounds into your room? It's a radio, of course!

A radio uses electricity to produce sound.

What Is Sound?

Sound is a kind of energy that causes our ears to hear things. It is produced when something vibrates, or moves back and forth very quickly. It travels in waves that move through the air like ripples on water. You cannot see these waves, but when they reach your ears, you can hear the sound.

The farther the waves travel, the weaker the sound becomes. Your ears cannot hear sounds that come from far away because they are too weak. That's why radios are useful.

 Sound waves can move easily through water. This scientist is dropping listening devices into the icy water to try to hear seals growling and whales singing!

How Does a Radio Work?

A radio captures sound waves from far away, changes them into electricity, and then changes them back into sounds that you can hear. At the radio station, sound waves are changed into electrical signals. The signals are carried on special radio waves that travel in all directions through the air.

This tower transmits radio waves through its antennas. People in the United States listen to radio stations, and people in Mexico listen to *estaciones de radio,* but the radio waves broadcast by these stations work in exactly the same way!

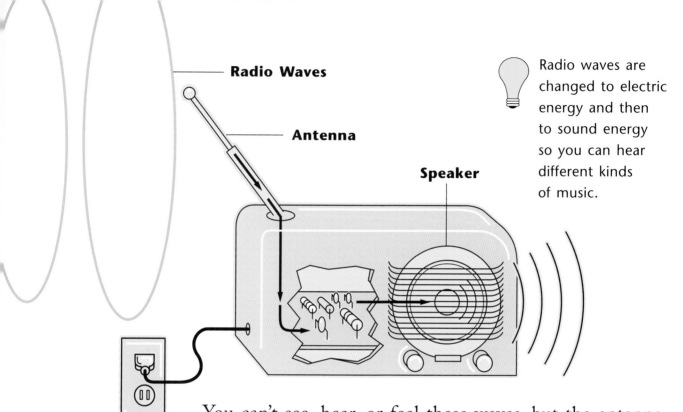

Radio Waves

Antenna

Speaker

Radio waves are changed to electric energy and then to sound energy so you can hear different kinds of music.

You can't see, hear, or feel these waves, but the antenna of your radio receives them. Your radio then changes the electrical signals into sound that you can hear, which comes to you through your radio's speakers.

Each station sends its own waves, and by turning the dial on your radio, you can receive waves from whatever station you want.

5

Heating Up!

How would you like to spend a long, cold winter without any heat in your home to warm you or to cook your food? It wouldn't take you long to realize how important heat is.

For thousands of years, people cooked their meals and warmed their homes with heat from a stove that worked like a fireplace. Now we get our heat from furnaces, radiators, and electric appliances (such as toasters and microwave ovens) that cook our food. We don't need to build a fire to have a hot meal—all we have to do is turn on a switch!

Some homes used stoves for warmth when it was cold. How do you heat your home?

What Is Heat?

Heat is a kind of energy created by tiny things called molecules that are moving very quickly. Heat always travels in one direction: from something warm to something cool. This happens because the fast-moving molecules in something warm bump into the slower-moving molecules in something cool, making the slow-moving molecules move more quickly. The quicker the molecules move, the warmer something becomes.

Heat energy flows from the hot teapot into the cool air.

Heat can be produced in different ways. Chemical reactions, like those that take place in our bodies when we eat, can produce heat. Friction, which occurs when one object is rubbed against another, can also produce heat.

A stove is one appliance that produces heat so that we can cook. How does your family cook dinner?

How Does a Popcorn Popper Work?

Many appliances, such as a popcorn popper, use electricity to produce heat. Like the thin wire in a lightbulb, a thin wire in the popcorn popper heats up as electricity flows through it, warming the air in the popcorn popper. A small fan blows the warm air up to the popcorn kernels, and the heat energy that is produced makes the kernels pop.

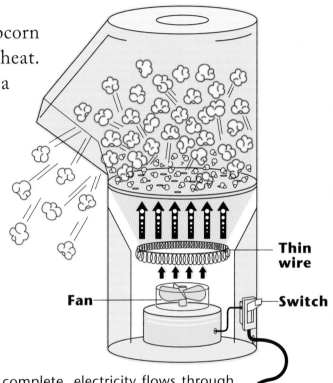

Thin wire

Fan

Switch

When this circuit is complete, electricity flows through the thin wire and changes electric energy to heat energy, warming these popcorn kernels until they pop!

How Can Magnets Help Us?

If you have ever stuck a piece of your artwork to the refrigerator door with a magnet, you have seen another powerful force at work. Magnets are pieces of metal, such as iron or steel, that can attract, or pull, certain other types of metal toward them. The attraction between a magnet and the steel in your refrigerator door holds your artwork in place. How does this powerful force called **magnetism** work?

Magnets can pick up many metal objects.

What Is Magnetism?

Magnetism is a force between objects that either pulls them together or pushes them apart. But how does that happen? The two ends of a magnet are called the magnet's north pole and south pole. When the north pole of one magnet is placed near the south pole of another, the two magnets are attracted to each other. However, if two north poles or two south poles are placed near each other, they repel, or push each other away.

 Opposite poles are attracted to each other.

 Like poles repel each other.

Some magnets called **electromagnets** can be created by using an electric current. Electromagnets are made by wrapping a wire many times around a piece of iron. When an electric current flows through the wire, the piece of iron becomes a magnet that attracts other metals. When the electricity stops flowing, the iron loses its magnetic power. When the electromagnet in a junkyard crane is turned on, the crane can pick up something as heavy as a car. When the electromagnet is turned off, the crane drops the object.

Powerful electromagnets are used to move heavy pieces of scrap metal in junkyards. What happens when the power is turned off?

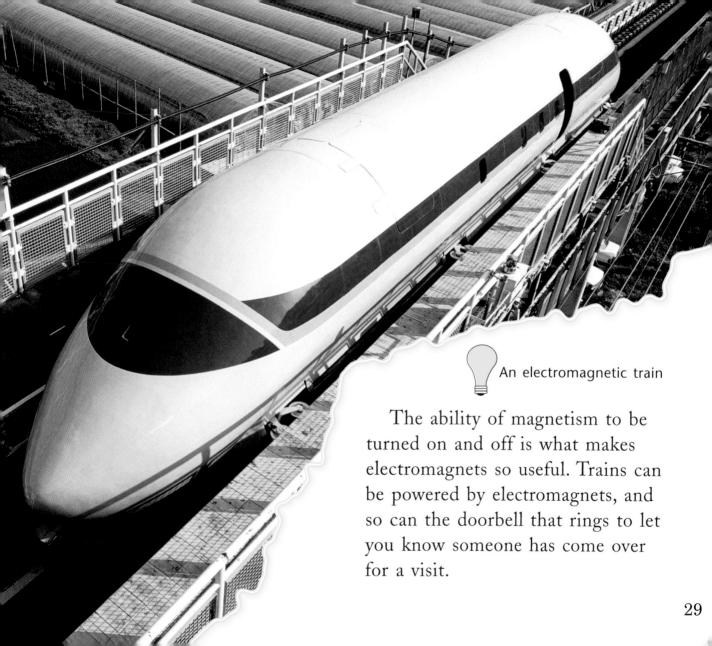

An electromagnetic train

The ability of magnetism to be turned on and off is what makes electromagnets so useful. Trains can be powered by electromagnets, and so can the doorbell that rings to let you know someone has come over for a visit.

How Does a Doorbell Work?

If you took a doorbell apart, you would find a small electromagnet inside that is part of an electrical circuit. When you press the doorbell button, the circuit is closed, and electricity flows through the coils of the electromagnet.

This closed circuit allows electricity to magnetize the electromagnet. Once magnetized, the electromagnet pulls toward a tone bar and strikes it, making the "ding" sound that you hear. When you let go of the button, the electromagnet stops being magnetized and bounces back against the other tone bar, making the "dong" sound.

Doorbell Button

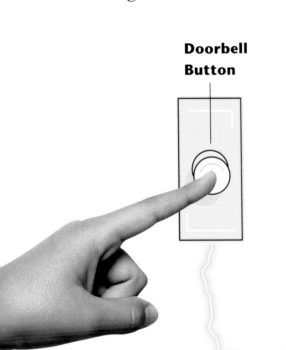

Power Source

Energy in Action

"Ding-dong!" The electric company has arrived at your home to tell your family that the power lines have been fixed. As the radio begins to play and the smell of popcorn fills the kitchen, you remember your new mystery book. Full of excitement, you turn on the lights, ready to read now that your energy source is back in action!

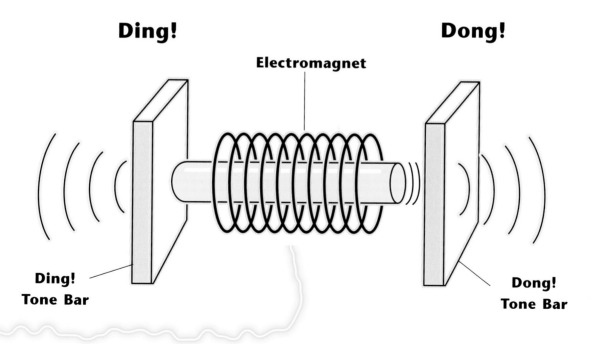

Ding!

Dong!

Electromagnet

Ding! Tone Bar

Dong! Tone Bar

⚡ Glossary ⚡

circuit the path of an electric current

electricity a form of energy found in nature and used to power many appliances

electromagnet a type of magnet that is created through the use of an electric current

energy the power of certain forces in nature to do work

friction the rubbing of one object against another

generator a machine that changes energy from a natural source into electricity

magnetism the power of a magnet to attract or repel other objects

solar energy power that comes from the sun

⚡ Index ⚡